I Pledge Allegiance

Michelle Jovin, M.A.

I can say the Pledge of Allegiance.

I pledge allegiance to the Flag
of the United States of America,
and to the Republic
for which it stands,
one Nation under God,
indivisible,
with liberty and justice for all.

I promise with my hand on my heart.

I pledge allegiance to the Flag of the United States of America, and to the Republic for which it stands, one Nation under God, indivisible, with liberty and justice for all.

People show allegiance.
They are loyal.

*I pledge allegiance to the Flag
of the United States of America,
and to the Republic
for which it stands,
one Nation under God,
indivisible,
with liberty and justice for all.*

A republic is the way the country is run. The flag is a symbol for the republic.

I pledge allegiance to the Flag
of the United States of America,
and to the Republic
for which it stands,
one Nation under God,
indivisible,
with liberty and justice for all.

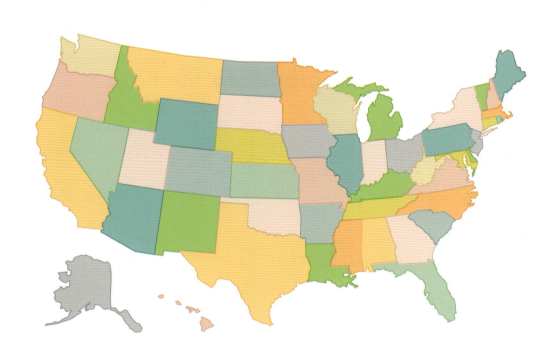

The nation is the country.

I pledge allegiance to the Flag
of the United States of America,
and to the Republic
for which it stands,
one Nation under God,
indivisible,
with liberty and justice for all.

The people are indivisible.
They stay together.

I pledge allegiance to the Flag
of the United States of America,
and to the Republic
for which it stands,
one Nation under God,
indivisible,
with liberty and justice for all.

Think and Talk

What does it mean to be free?

The people have freedom.

I pledge allegiance to the Flag
of the United States of America,
and to the Republic
for which it stands,
one Nation under God,
indivisible,
with liberty and justice for all.

The people want fairness.

I pledge allegiance to the Flag of the United States of America, and to the Republic for which it stands, one Nation under God, indivisible, with liberty and justice for all.

Jump into Fiction

The Pledge

Each child puts their right hand over their heart. They take a deep breath.

Then, they begin.
"I pledge allegiance to the flag," they say.

Civics in Action

There are many ways we can show love for the country. We can say the pledge. We can wear red, white, and blue.

1. Have a red, white, and blue day at your school.

2. Wear the colors. Put up posters and flags.

3. Say the pledge. Sing songs about the country.